Christmas 1995

To Gail —
May
"inner happiness"
while reading this
book. The author has
Shaker roots. Enjoy!
Love,
Laura + Kent

DANCING
IN THE
WIND

JOYCE W. POVOLNY

William Sessions Limited
The Ebor Press
York, England

ISBN 1 85072 161 0

Printed in 10 on 12 point Helvetica Typeface by
William Sessions Limited
The Ebor Press
York, England

To Mojmir

Without whom I would be just
a wind-blown dancer.

My heart is a poet
Though less sublime
Than the ancient bards
Of cadence and rhyme.

CONTENTS

CONTENTS *cont.*

CONTENTS *cont.*

RELIGION

Weep Not for Abraham
(Variation on Genesis 22)

And it came to pass after these things
That God did tempt Abraham
And said unto him, Abraham: and he said
Behold, here I am.
And he said, Take now thy son
Thine only son, Isaac,
Whom thou lovest,
And get thee unto the land of Moriah;
And offer him there for a burnt offering
Upon one of the mountains
Which I will tell thee of.

And they came to the place
Which God had told him of; and
Abraham built an altar there,
And laid the wood in order, and
Bound Isaac, his son,
And laid him on the altar upon the wood.

And Abraham stretched forth his hand,
And took the knife to slay his son.

Then God stopped time
And in the instant between
One heartbeat and the next
Poured eternity down the tears
Of a trembling Hebrew,
('Here am I, Lord'),
Prefiguring His own agony
In the burnt offering of Father and Son.

Weep not for Abraham;
For him there was a ram.
But weep for God:
In Him the knife of Abraham
Fell home.

1965
Friends Journal

When Jesus therefore saw her weeping and the Jews also weeping which came with her, he groaned in spirit and was troubled.

(John 1:33)

Lazarus, Come Forth

He wept not for Lazarus' fate
Nor for their mourning tears
But that their blinded eyes
Had sealed him in a stone-cold tomb.

"Lazarus, come forth and show
The alabaster flesh of man
When winding clothes are loosed
And fall away."

He groaned in his travail
To make plain
The eye deceives the mind
Which running on from th' event
To an imaginary fate.
Holds him helpless captive there
In unconfirmed belief.

"Lazarus, come forth and show
The alabaster flesh of man
When winding clothes are loosed
And fall away."

And he that was dead came forth
Reborn.
His limbs were loosed to life
And his face unmarred by death.

Then the Lord of life commanded them and said:
"Behold this man renewed
Whose destined end reviews
Before your startled eye
Man triumphant whole in One."

"Behold this man! Remember me!
Death deludes you, fearful souls.
When mind-created word is split
And life is seen supreme
The eye perceives as mind:
They see as one
And death to death is done."

1981
Friends Journal

Canticle of Preliminary Praise

O Thou lovely beyond our canticles of praise
How yet shall the heart song's stunned silence
Frame for all to see the burden of love
Which ripens for Thee?
(Do we even dare use the "Thee" familiarly?
Yet Thou sayest!)

The eye of the worshipper which perceives
In every bud of tentative and of powerful love,
And in every delicate tendril of far-away fauna and flora
The unfolding of the unimaginable Imagination
Of the Most Serene and the Most Secret Being
Who is like the unchallengeable yet present dome
Of the warm and the liquid night sky
With luminous clouds (Whence the light?)
Passing, passing, in slow relief,
Over its unconcerned black background.
(Isn't it the unconcern of its absolute control?)

Ah, the vapors are like the generations of human hieroglyphs
Which glide over the ever-glowing Face,
Whose substance is always the same,
Yet whose shifting conformations
With their gossamer trails,
Are of infinite fascination
To the expert and the practised eye of the Artist.
Black and white –
The contrast sets them off in bold relief.

Canticle of Preliminary Praise *cont.*

The eye of the worshipper,
Perceiving all this,
Is half-closed in modest reserve,
Not daring the bold stare
Of the uninitiated
Upon the Perfect Passion whose possibilities
Stretch infinitely far away into the interstellar spaces
Beyond the measures and calculations of our frail thought.
Yet who lays out His wares in the market place of His world
For all our immediate rejoicing.

In the end, as Canticles of Preliminary Praise,
We can only fall down with our Father, Job,
And like him, murmur,
"Who, who of us measures the wind?"
And burying our naked, wet, sweet and savory faces
In the brown and succulent earth,
Remain prostrate now and forevermore
In our small, dumb, corners
Of adoration.

1982
Fox Cry

To be an Instrument of The Lord is My Desire

To be an instrument of the Lord is my desire.
To let His truth flow through me
Unimpeded by my desires
Is my ambition.
O great love,
No man hath greater love
Nor instrument more finely tuned
Than this.
Nor at one point easily broken
Nor at another broken at all.
I am finely tuned;
But as yet I need a bow;
I cannot sing by myself.
But as yet I need a bow
To break my strings
And then I shall sing alone.

1971
Friends Journal

The Great Joy, Exquisite and Unutterable

Dear God,
You give me exactly what I need,
Not what I want
Whether I want it or not.
Thy will be done
Whether we will it or not.

Indeed,
Thou art marvelous beyond words,
Thou terrible One
In Thy austere and delicate beauty
Which is so far beyond the frail wails
That we divine bards must invent
In utter and dumb-founded amazement
And offer as our minute lullabies
To soothe Thy dreaming labors.
In the end, as all is each, echoing, sung,
Cosmic silence will be
Our only final testament of honor.
How else shall we worship properly?

To begin. If then, I utter now
The tiniest, timid,
"I am willing"
To be a small song
As chant-offering
Before Thy alabaster altar
In the holy sanctuary of Thy present Being,
Thy old, conditional Covenant,
Fixed between Thee and the Patriarchs,
Its lovely logo,
The painted rainbow which binds together
The storm-bound sky,
Still holds true for me, iron-bound.
But yet it is as unconditional as ever
From the first day beyond remembrance.

Thy archaic law of Love,
Fluid and exact – ever the **most** exacting – labor law
(As laws tend to be today)

Is revealed to us
By the Advent of Thy surety-bound-servant-soul,
Jesus Christ of Bethlehem, Judea,
In his holy, human temple,
And binds by the same vow
Unto death, which binds not
For sight of the shimmering green fields
Of present and yet-to-be-Paradise
And is constructed of the delicate, unseen,
Titanium filament of faith in Love,
Gossamer thread only to the eye
Of the uncommitted.

The vow is irrevocable from the moment
Of the taking of the principal, primary choice,
Done far away beyond the mists of our present memory
When we stood as empty chalices
(Unformed except in eternal Essences
Wafted from fields of Flowers
Afar even before time was Chaos)
Before the throne of God
And He freely offered us
Out of pity and most tender love,
"Choose, you, my little children,
Whom you will be of Me
And where and when."
And we pointed to our particular crystal-colored wines
With joy beyond endurance
With all its fruity expectations.
He then closed our greedy and dazzled eyes
And planted us in his vineyard to ripen slowly
Through eons of aging
Into the final burst of bouquet
(Ah! Those heady perfumes . . .)
When we become the new wine
Of our old, original first taste
And are drunk with delight as
The chalice shimmers libation –
Holy Grail of Heaven from Thee

The Great Joy – *cont.*

Are we become the Body and Blood,
The living Holy Sacrament, flowing
As we love one another freely
As He loves us in forming sinew and divine cell.
Each **sui generis**, and all outward body
So inward Thee, consciously, the members every one,
Each in time passing through the filter
Of the eternal Now,
The Body of Christ is swelling, burgeoning,
Through time immemorial, **ad infinitum**, away, away
Into the nether far reaches of the space
And time concepts
Of the imagining dreams of the original Will of Delights
For the crown of creation, the ultimate lovers,
The worshippers,
Hymn-singers of infinite ingenuity, all.
Ah! Man and Woman, Adams and Eves of
Endless inventive praising,
Return, please.

For me, the new wine is to be
A daughter of Zion.
She of the gray morning,
Walking into the December mist,
On the day of the Barred Owl.

Whispering to the listening ear
And trembling
Like the last leaf on an autumn oak,
"Whither Thou has gone,
My God and My Lord,
My Redeemer,
Savior of my soul,
If Thou wilt,
So will I, too, go."
But, before I go
I will, in bridling, ask
Of each one,
"Who art thou? And whence comest thou?

The Great Joy – *cont.*

And whither goest thou?
Anywhere?
Knowest thou, my child?"

And I will ask,
Reining in
Yet again,
"Dost thou, too,
Wish to come Home,
Home,
Home,
To the patiently awaiting
Breasts of Love?"
And finally,
For me
In secret silence
At home
The perpetual peace
Of contemplation.
That is the promise
And God does not lie
Nor do I.

1982

Love and Justice

I have gyrated, tipsy with the effort,
Down the long convoluted descending corridors of our
Judicious legal system
Whose harsh doors are marked, nevertheless,
With the various once-only notations
Of their particular presiding chief justice
And I have sought ever to be its only and always ever
Perfectly blinded balancer.

But I perceive now
As I stroll in the cool, lavender-shadow, evening
In the presence of our king Lord
And we muse together by the shores of the
Ever-violet-streams of Life

That by pure, animal, instinct
We've always known, haven't we,
My lovely children?
That love is all our
And even our only all every perfectly
Balanced ultimate justice.

1984

Coriander and Cardamom

At twenty, it's rosemary and thyme;
Salt and pepper wisdom at thirty-three.
At forty, oregano and marjoram,
At fifty, coriander, cardamom and turmeric;
At sixty, frankincense and myrrh,
And seventy, sealed in a stone-cold tomb
To await again the seed-time
Of rosemary and thyme
Whose tassles blow on the summer wind
Roots suckled in the gloom.

1964

Prayer

Obedience to the Lord
Is a taut and singing string
And I am exhausted from listening.
Turn now Thy Face away from me, O Lord,
That I may no more hear Thee
And rest.

1966

Father S, A Timeless Chaplain

Gentle on the mountaintop
Are the feet of him
Who bringeth peace,
His everlasting covenant
With the Lord of mercy
Is his daily resurrection –
A just recompense
For him who dared to pray.

1966

Let Thine Eye be Single

The single eye!
Let it sing
In its multi-colored forms
The song of the prism.

1969

The Prophet and The Saint

And when he had done his harangue among the people
He saw the saint and signalled him to wait.
"I must have words with you
For I fear we work at odds
To fulfill our Father's end."

The Prophet angrily then
Accused the Saint:
"I cry God's wrath upon their heads
Make straight the Way of the Lord
To test the stalwart-limbed
And winnow out the frail.
But you pity their travail
And with tender looks and murmuring mercy
You vitiate my word!

You make them irresponsible
By excusing their transgressions
On the grounds of human frailty.
One must seek the nature of the lesion first
Before applying healing balm
As you do without inquiring
The nature of the sin.
Your love absorbs the evil
And returns it a purifièd physic
To mend the momentary breach
In harmony.

My heart is closed as a stone
On whom the people stand;
Yours the living waters
Of a mountain stream.
We must go hand in hand
If we expect the people
To be recalled from hell."

The Prophet and The Saint *cont.*

The Prophet, wearied, sank down, drawn,
Upon the scorching rocks.
The Saint undid the leather thong
Of his goat-skin water flask
And gave the man to drink.
"A prophet admonishes
A saint ministers
And each his appointed task performs
To bring 'round the holy circle
Of absolution.

And when you have gained your strength
Come bide the night with me
Ere you begin tomorrow's labors."

1969

Soul Force

Out of the mandala in your breast
Comes the truth.
The direction of your destiny
Like solar flares
Enters your awareness.

1969
Friends Journal

Greatness is a Spiral

Greatness is a spiral
Toward simplicity.
Implicitly.
Alpha and Omega writes
In a child-like script
That the kaleidoscope
Is a simple instrument.

1969

The Rainbow: A Variation on Genesis 9:11-17

Dear God,
Accept our tears
Which, if shed,
Would drown the mighty seas
That girdle the world
And swing to and fro on tide time.
These would be still pools
In the wooded sanctuary
Of your heart, O Lord,
If you do not accept
The oblation of our tears
And thereby wake to see the bow
Arched over your perfect creation,
Signifying a perpetual covenant
Between the quick and the dead.

1969

The Quick occupy Sheol

Does it ever occur to you
That we walk the by-ways
Of Sheol now, our long-lost sins
Seeking redemption?
Until again we take
The well-known trip,
Shooting the rapids of the river Styx
Until by lottery our number's up
And we see things
A far cry from earth.

1969

The Chase

Delicate as a flower
Is the Lord
Though less ephemeral than the summer grass
Which withereth in the autumn winds.
To catch Him put away vanity
For the Lord hateth a proud man.
What thinkest thou
That thou canst do without the Lord?
He is very nigh thee
As the wild flower of the meadow
Which thou seest not
For searching the heavens.
Bend, stoop, pick,
For the beautiful is the commonest thing
Neglected by the blind wanderer.

1970

Purged

Stripped of all haughtiness,
I stand before Thee.
Naked of all desires,
I present myself unto Thee.
Raise me up, I pray Thee,
For Thou alone art King.
Let me follow Thee.
Shorn as I am,
To the uttermost parts of the sea
Or to hell.
Let me be faithful and chaste,
Dead to earthly delights.
Let the trumpet sound
And I shall present myself,
A soldier without arms,
As was Christ, clay yet divine.
Send me, I pray Thee,
For I seek the dead among the living
To lead them as Christ did
To heights they once knew
Before they were born.

1970

Premeditated Verdict

You look through a glass darkly,
Ever unaware that the blood your claws draw
Is the same color as your own.
You feel only your own pain,
Not knowing the venom you spit
Wounds equally.
Are you guilty then
Of what you do not perceive?
No. Blind giants are ever acquitted.
Are you, however, forgiven?
Yes. But only by those unattached to you.
Our linked hate tips the balance scale
Making justice impossible
In your old age.
We, the wounded, are rather guilty
While you go free, paying no debt,
Bearing no burden.
Till on Judgment Day
Your test will come
And then shall we see
No justice done
But if love outweigh animosity.

1970

Hell

Hell is nowhere.
It is caught, the web of your sins,
In the sinews of your mind.
Torn from your limbs
As the light went out.
You float like a man-o-war
In the nebulous net of the universe
With no way back.
Full of penance,
There is no flesh and bone,
No warm blood to spill
For the sake of the wronged.
Your skull is gone, no brain to break
In retribution to the innocent
You have caught in your net of guile.
There is no way to righteousness.
The ghostly wind booms,
A companion to your anguish.
Your cry for silence
Is heard only by the ticking of the time bomb
Whose hour you do not know.
It will blow you to dust.
But be calm. Your particles will form a new star.

1970

Before Time Was

In the beginning, before time was,
We chose our destiny
As God laid out the panoply
Of possibilities
And said: "Now choose."

1970

Mysterium Tremendum

I loom over the horizon,
Deus ex machina.
Am I?

Reply.

1970

Alone

Smithy, grasp the iron bar
And stoke the fire with it.
Hammer it red-hot over
The flange of the anvil.
Twist it, turn it, burn, crush
And bruise it till it
Satiates your hunger.
Plunge it glowing into the water
And take no note
Of the hiss and sigh
Of the wrought-iron ikon.
O, glance once to satisfy your soul
And let it go.
Plunging downward, falling, falling,
Watch it weep and wail
For home.
Watch as it rips the earth;
The clash of elements is terrific.
Spiralling up in every finer circles
Watch for a thousand nights
The fireworks. Take heed, however,
The heat is beyond bearing.
The lesser metal copies but cannot,
Cannot, cannot. Take heed
Of the boomerang lest Thy mercy
Be too late and the flaming earth erupt,
A final testament to Thy errant judgment.

1970

Numinous Night

Tender is the night.
A quiet moon white in earth and sky alike.
The crickets creak
And an occasional bird peeps.
The lonely hoot of a train in the distance
Haunts the stillness for a moment
Leaving in its trail long memories
As I sit in the silence imbibing peace
And the sense of the numinous unknown
Looms in the black and white velvet sky
Of a midnight in May.

1970

Hymn Maker

Do not be afraid that Silence
Is the only way
To express the Silent!
O, inexhaustible man,
Hymn maker of infinite ingenuity,
"Beauty" is only the beginning
Of thy celestial vocabulary!

1970

The Chosen

Are not the Jews an allegory?
Their to and fro
Toward and away from God
The image of us all
And of each of us
To reach the heavenly center
Where all is still
And we meet in truth,
Allegory discarded?

1970

Alpha and Omega

My desire beats against the window
Of my soul
Like the wings of a frantic dove
Who, when it falls exhausted,
Leaves the pane unmarred, unmoved –
The same as ever.

O Mysterious One
I did not perceive
That despair and faith are alike.
And,
That in the grave of desire
Lies the cradle of knowledge.

1972
Friends Journal

Anachronism Used

In every era there are those few who
Salt the age when ancient savor and
Who, when the pendulum swings out too far
And hangs suspended, quivering,
On the fatal stroke,
Deflect the fall
And change the hours upon the Face
And bring the minds of men around again
Upright.

1973
Friends Journal

Dialogue with Jehovah after Psalm 130

Out of the depths have I cried
Unto Thee, O Lord.
Lord, hear my voice:
Let thine ears be attentive
To the voice of my supplications.
Have pity on me
And make it impossible for me
To disobey Thee.

"Silence", He replied.
"Cans't Thou not see?
I am Christ crucified.
Follow me."

1973

Shadow-Force

Winding down the staircase of my life,
I catch a glimpse of you,
Shadow-force, at every corner.
You stand in stone,
The eyes only alive and piercing.
You beckon to me without a motion
But I am afraid of those fierce eyes,
Cool, calculating, fixed on me.
If I were to come
Would I find comfort
Or only discipline?
This is the trauma, the enigma,
Before every surrender.
Uncertain of the magic one.
Shall I, too, pass by with eyes downcast,
Avoiding?

1975

Consolation

The beam through the prism
Sprinkles us over the green earth
To lie fallow or fit
For progression from the divine
To the mortal dimension.
Weep not, therefore, fragment,
For you and you alone
Fill up full the Father's pleasure –
A perfect mosaic of Himself.

1975

The Arroyo

If I promise one thing
Will you give me back my poetry.
The rolling rush of water
Out of my bloody youth?

If I promise one thing
Will the bone-dust arroyo
Boil again over the brink
Of crucible clay?

If I promise one thing
Will you visit me
In the starfire hours
With music for certain ears?

Will you seize me again
And crack my joints
With the jar of melody
From subterranean source?

If I promise one thing
Will you promise one thing?
I know you will
But will I?

I must promise one thing
I hear in secret
Or the arroyo awaiting the rain
Will inch by inch
Fill with silt
And like an ill-tended grave
Sink slowly from sight

O save me.
O cleanse.
O dight!

1980

Pursuit

Hound of Heaven, you pursue me
Up and down the labyrinth
Of my subterfuges to escape you.
Yet the moment I lie down to rest,
In one bound you are upon me
And I am devoured.

1980

The Season of The Passion

The fresh-flower season is upon us again,
The season of the Passion.
When birds sang freely,
The wind sparkled on Galilee
And the sun sailed hot in the sky,
Death stalked our Savior.
Blood-sweat dappled the new grass in Gethsemane
As he prayed for the cup of sorrow to pass.
Nevertheless, not my will,
And he went wounded to the grave.
But on the third day rose again
And purchased with his life eternal spring.
As we tell and retell the tale
Unto all generations to come dancing
Down time's byways
In the season of the gentle rains.

1980

Peace

What dark forces stir thy soul
To make thee a martyr of black blood?
What evils lurk in thy entrails
To turn thy face from love?
Ever thus thou hast been.
No joy lightens thy travail.
With anguish thou dost tread
Thy lonely way.
Thou dost refuse all succor,
Preferring to steep in the sleepless night
Of thy disturbèd dreams.
Yet waiting for thee as with all others
Is He who would redeem thee
From thy benighted plight.
Patiently He calls thee.
Hear thou Him who died for thy sins.
Turn at this remote hour
To Him who would give thee rest
From thy weary path.
Let the living God seize thee
And awake from thy hapless reverie.
Come dream of Him in thy waking hours
And surely He will not let thee perish
In thy peristent folly.
Await the Savior, He overcame the world
And He will conquer the seven devils
Who besiege thee.
He who made thee will redeem thee
And turn again thy face toward peace.
Not the peace of the world
But the peace which overcame the world
Even for those so lost as thee.

1980

Preliminaries and Finalities

Down the holy tears of desire
Pours salvation.
Across the waterfall of unmitigated want
Sounds the trump of glory.
What does one see
After all secondary sightings fade?
A clear vision of a rose aureole at dawn,
Crowning the shining corpus.
And a rainbow burning in the night sky.
And one laughs with the dissolution of meaning
And joy is absolute.

1982

In the Reliquary of Thy Holy Stone Altar
the Roundelay of the Butterfly

I have sung thee a new song
And have brushed thy lips with it.
Gentle as a butterfly opens
It flutters, wet-winged,
In the pulsating inner-sanctury
Of thy still-devout child's heart
Which is as yet, of course,
Out of a desperate necessity,
The closed-stone cocoon
        of
            thy
               untried
                  youth.

Thou art to see,
      If thou wilt
           wait with me,
That it is
      a
         gift
            from me
            from thee
To the most reserved of the inner sancta.
The reliquary of thy holy stone altar,
      The World's Soul.

1983

The Wings of the Dove or Duodescent

The wings of the dove
Sing,
Sing,
To me

Out of the Bliss of Eternity
Where there I am
Remembering me
Sitting on the limb of the Ancient Tree
Where there was I
And will recall to thee
The work of the word's simultaneity.

In the ancient hum of the mystery
How we suddenly discovered what was not
And now it ever shall be
The whortle in the dove of the wings to thee.
While here I am
Remembering Me
Alight on the limbs of the Ancient Tree
Where there was I
Remembering Me
Singing like a dove
As it sings to thee
Out of the Bliss of Eternity
The sound in our song's perpetuity.

When we listen we hear
Singularly
Out of the Bliss of Eternity
Where we descended not once but twice
Duocentrally
Out of the Bliss of Eternity
Which the wings of the dove
Are reminding thee

The Wings of the Dove or Duodescent *cont.*

Is the descent of the One
In the multiplicity
By whose light is absorbing
Their shadows in simplicity.
Where I am prepared for thee
To sing in the Bliss of Eternity.

1985

"Whortle" is a new word derived from "whirl" and "vortex" which are based on the Latin word "vertere" which means "to turn". "Vertere" related to the OHG word "werden" or "to become". The word "whortle" denotes the way I receive the new word which came up to my mind from the source of all in the center of the breast as a kind of whirlwind-up-from-the vortex and is the sound that the wings of the mourning dove makes when it flies.

"Duodescent" is a new word which appeared in my mind as descriptive of the creative process. It means the interstice, the instant in time and event, where a human being and God discover and create together simultaneously.

The Winds of Time

The winds of time sweep 'round
The curves of the universe
And on in around again within us.
They come out of the Soul of the Holy One
Whose Being is Time in winds external
Whose Soul is Time of winds internal
And being One so being none
But the winds of Time that never cease
And never run.

1985

The Watcher and the Watched

Consciousness is like the Sea
Watching its own particularities
Of which each one of us Key
Therefore, everyone is free
Which is God's responsibility!

1985

The Flaming Sword of Paradise

I am the flaming sword of Paradise
Which pierces your side
Even in times of milk and honey;
Or an angel who comforts you with the Annunciation.
I am the rock
And, at the same time, a crevice.
I invite you to fall into me and drown.
Or come unto me with lips sealed with a burning coal
And unshod feet.
It is all the same to me;
For I shall requite you of all iniquity
For I am the flaming sword of Paradise
Which pierces your side
Even in times of milk and of honey
And out of me shall flow forevermore
The living waters of eternal life.

1985

Penultimate
A Conundrum of Time and Event

The pendulum swings back
On the penultimate stroke.
It never moves
O Kali and Vishnu!

1985

Wish-fulfillment

The wind in the trees blows of me
Sailing beyond permissible perimeters.
Full-roiling, I will be Thee.
Still,
I have asked.
Thou has given
The unnavigable sea.

1985

Answer

I once asked God
In a rage
Over the agonized
Dying
Of a beautiful and pure woman.
"What do you want?"
When the weeping trailed away
With the rising sound of the water
And wood
And I was still
The answer came,
"Nothing".
I was silent
And open-spaced
Before perfection,
Lost in the meadow of awe.

1985
Friends Journal

The Inviolate: Hymn

When souls unveil to Inner Sun
The ringing bells when thus begun
Will ring in inner harmony
Inviolate in humanity.

They swell the peal and thus release
The golden songs of joy and peace,
Concordant strains that hail from Thee
In their eternal purity.

When we appear as Bells of Thee
Who then am I and who are we?
But singers in the melody
Composed of light and love by Thee.

They say that it cannot be done
But tolling voices now begun
Will sing Thy hallowed harmony,
Thy love within humanity.

Illuminate us, Deity,
Thou Construct of humanity,
In which resides the melody,
The gift of love that comes from Thee
Which we will hear repeatedly
If we proceed so candidly
As lovely bells that had begun
When souls unveiled before the Sun.

Comprehension

Judgment reads what all others
Read in a face,
A one-dimensional view
And then
Condemnation.

Love reads the complexity
Behind the mask.
It shines on the turn of the coin
And illumines the close-guarded vault
Of the most secret soul.
It softens the sorrow
Drawn in the corners of eyes
And knows
That the particular style of compromise
Tells its secret, too.

1960

LOVE

For My Father

O value the man much
For despite his decrepitude
And many sins
He has loved much
And forgiven all.
At the end of the road
Let him see the light
Of forgiveness on Thy countenance, O Lord.
Let him blaze forth
In his original beauty
After the final curtain is drawn
On his mortal remains.
Let him come before Thy throne in glory
For he has been faithful ever
To the dreams of childhood.

1960

Presentness

Did ever you feel the perfume of a soul
Who is distant from you
Yet present in your heart?
He is far yet his soul is closeted
Within your own
Exuding his essence
For your life and breath to enjoy.
Breathing him in is rapturous
For he is nearer perhaps
Than when he is present.
Love is the catalyst,
The luminous shadow in which
He comes to being within you.
Cherish the soul and don't speak of it
To anyone
Lest they laugh
And he evaporate,
Leaving you desolate.

1965

Lovely as the Dew

Lovely as the dew
Are you
But evanescent,
No hint of amaranth
In hue.

1970

Science

She loved him with her whole force and energy.
He died.
She fell down dumb,
Her mind shattered.
Maladjusted personally, the psychiatrist said.
Damn the omniscient blind!
Of what else did she die
Than a broken soul?

1970

First Love

Gracious and lovely as a lily are you
That I dare not approach you openly.
From a distance I feast on your beauty,
You are my first love
And profound it is.
I would not pluck you now
But only silently admire
You bending on your supple stalk.

1970

Lovely as a Shadow

Lovely as a shadow
Of the tamarind tree
Are you.
Light and airy though leafy
Do I perceive you
Through the husk
That covers your inner soul.
Delicate are you
And difficult as a shadow
To grasp.
But I would have it
No other way
As I approach you
Through the tangle
Of your subterranean roots.

1970

Old Men in the Spring

Old men in the spring blow about bewildered
Who they are or where they've been.
They stand at street corners with rheumy eye
And flopping pants.
Too proud to ask for help. Too shy,
They cross alone.

Old man in the spring,
Doddering half blind down the lime-green lane
Will you turn around just once more
To see me weep?

No, you will not
For you have already gone 'round a corner
And severed all connections with men.
The lime-green lane is your element now
And it hails you welcome
As I bid you farewell.

1973
Friends Journal

The Tryst

I will never forget,
As you have already,
Our tryst at the river's edge.
I was old, as women are wont to be,
And so my memory was even then long.
But you, you were a child
In my hand.
Yet our spirits touched
And fused, one sun, one star.
And we became ageless for a moment
Long ago by the Afton's banks.

1980

The Unfolding

Thrusting through pretenses,
I come upon you,
Hollow-eyed, stalwart,
Yet quivering.
One thing I've learnt in life
Is not to be surprised by surprises
And thus I have you.
Lambent with light,
Complete, bone-white, trusting,
Frightened yet holding your ground,
You appear nascent
And what joy I take
In your white birth.

1980
Bardic Echoes

Advice to the Lovelorn

Play to Me, saith the Lord,
And I will pierce his ear
With the swelling song of the universe
Which sings through all the generations from Adam
And Eve.
Murmuring, vibrating, through all time
In a low key,
Whose melody, nevertheless, delights the ear
Of her who would hear
And whose disparate harmonies resolved
In a visible tone
When the Star shone.

1982

Mona Lisa

How a myriad of men
Have fallen before thee,
O Mona Lisa,
For the trifle of thy smile.
But is it a trifle?
Promise there is
Of passion
Beyond woman's guile.
Thou dost query
With faint lips
Who is worthy
Of the ocean
Beyond the hint?
Who of you
Will give me all?
For less I remain
An enigma, a mere slayer of men,
In my search.
 My lips will open for no less a man
Than I am woman.
My eye seals none
But an equal slayer.
Ask of me no less
And I shall reveal at last
More than a question
But full-flood bloom,
A high-tide summer's noon.

1983

Holy Unction

The vapor of your soul
drifts
like
dark
rose
smoke,
holy and benificent,
over my upturned breasts.

1985

INNER STRUGGLE

There are in Me Two Natures

There are in me two natures,
One, haughty, proud and disdainful.
The blood of ancient royalty runs in me
And I feel myself a cool queen –
An obscure heritage from I know not where
But strong, strong in me.
The other is the mystic and the metaphysician,
The struggle for
Cosmic understanding and humility.
But the former is too strong
And rules me:
And the face I show the world
Is the bitter struggle
To melt the pride of one
With the power of the other.

Is it a struggle between a given nature
And a learned nature,
Between experience and knowledge?
Or is it a struggle –
Between two given natures
In the same personality?
Did I learn pride or was it born in me?

I suppose Eve posed the same question
When the gates of Paradise closed!

1955

This is called Adjustment

Huckster of mediocrity,
Salesman of the status quo,
I hate you!
Yet I buy all your wares
Out of cowardice.

1965

Retrospective

O fight for your dreams.
Keep fresh mirrored in memory
The taunts, you, O tortured youth, flung at life.
Let not the agues of age
Rust your ambitions
For perfection.
Remain, white-haired giant,
God's favorite pupil
And He will spare you
A bent back and weighted heart.
Fresh will flash your eye.
Keen the gleam of your smile.
And out of the dross of ninety years
Will perpetually flow
Ever elusive youth –
The one you knew not
When you were but a stripling.

1970

Still

Still as a candle
Under a glass bell,
My soul.

When the storm shatters the wood
And shakes its black thunder
And rip-cord lightning,
Still as a candle
Under a glass bell,
My soul.

The hail beats 'gainst it
And bounds away
To no avail.
Still as a candle
Under a glass bell,
My soul.

The spring rain comes,
Spatters down,
Still as a daffodil
In the sun,
My soul.

1972
Friends Journal

Despair

It is like dragging the starved bones
Of your body through the burning sands
Of the Sahara of your soul.
There is no oasis;
Only the platinum-white sun,
The pitiless sand,
And the skeleton of a serpent
Dragging itself up the next dune,
Claw after claw, by instinct struggling
To sight the shimmering water.
But there is none – not even a mirage.
Only the sun and lifeless sand
Undulating on
Mile after mile forever.
That is despair: there is no end,
No break anywhere.

1973
Friends Journal

Drifting

Drifting across the salt-brine sea.
I will come to thee,
Languidly, in my own way.
Allow me room to maneuver.
Don't shout at me across the water
Which way the shore;
I know it.
But I must come at my own pace,
Slowly through the shoals,
Or not at all.

1975

Degrees of Dying

Dear Husband,
Once again I have betrayed you
While your love propped my heart
To try another man.
And this time the offense
So serious that
To pay it required full measure.
Therefore, I sleep
Perchance to dream.
Aye, is it so?
I search the heavens
And the earth
And the Great One
To answer "perchance."
But none sees me
For my eyes are sealed
In a black death mask.
I did not perceive
That for such as I
There is no second chance
And now it is beyond perceiving;
I lie burning and fallow
Now and forevermore.
Aye, it is so.

1975

The Hiatus

I was struck dumb
By the death of a wish.
You, my hope, to whom I spoke
Strode away
And the water-lily of my heart closed.
My ear closed
And my eye saw only forms,
Not connections.
You were the web
On whom I as spider spun
My metaphysical mysteries.
You were the tender chord
On whom I played
M y melancholy tunes.
Or like a water beetle
I skittered across the limpid surface
Of your quick humor.
The glance of an eye sufficed
For fusion.
Alas, the tension was too much
And we sundered.
I lay like a parched bone
In the desert
Until one day in early spring
I became aware of a listener

The Hiatus *cont.*

And a speaker who was not distant
From me
But lay fallow, the root connection
To the water-lily feeding me still
Under the opaque pond.
I was speaking to a false listener,
A reed in the wind, a sun-shadow,
Only an ear not a trumpet, too.
The water flower opened,
Fertile, and spread its pollen
Again. This time for anyone
With ear to listen and eye to see.
Not dead, but dormant.
Never dead, only sleeping
Under the weight of a false wish –
The wish to speak to one hearer only
And not to whomever is led
Up the rainbow path of my soul.

1978

When

Have I no more to say
Like the lilting song of yore,
The light shaft out of a roiling youth?
No more. My thoughts are darker now.
Too much has passed my way
To sing with carefree swing.
My passions are painted gray
And light is filtered through a faulty heart.
I have seen too much death,
My own notwithstanding.
I have prayed but have yet to see
My God face to face.
Though I have passed through the gates of hell
Not unscathed.
My hope is ever the same,
But doubt now rules as once did joy.
I have yet to see my God face to face.
When O Lord? How long I pray,
Trembling like an ancient Jew
Before a temple of silence.

1980

Peniel for Rachel

The austerities of the night are awesome.
Out of the bosom of the dark
The silence speaks
Whose light reveals Rachel wrestling with the angel.
Dawn comes, finds them both lying exhausted,
Rigid with grief.
A crow calls.

1982

Peniel [Penuel] is the place in the Old Testament (Genesis 32:30) where Jacob wrestles all night
with the angel. In the morning the angel smote Jacob in the thigh and said Jacob would be called
Israel from then on. Jacob called the place 'Peniel' because God had blessed him there. Rachel
was Jacob's wife.

The Dumb Tongue Flew

And the dumb tongue flew
Free from its captivation
In self-contemplation.
And what did it say?
It said it sang
Of the little birch tree
All hung in gold.
The color of its sap,
The same inside as out,
The apex of every man's dream.

1983

NATURE

Ah

I looked at the blooming white clouds
One summer afternoon
And bowed my head
And did not say what they were like
For excess of joy
And trembling fear
At the beginning of disintegration within
From looking right on
At a perfect thing.

1962

November Fen

A November fen
Is shattered oak
Brooding bronze
In onyx water.

1969

The Birch Tree

Come hand me your mysteries
That flow from the deep.
You leap in the sunlight
And hang in the gloom
Of a passing cloud-shadow
Come hand me your mysteries
That come from the deep.
I, too, want to flow in your current.

1969
Friends Journal

Fling Up the Shutters of Spring

Fling up the shutters of spring!
And sing out your song
On the new wind.
Come, Daffodil, trumpet in the sun!
Tulip, stretch forth your petals toward the sky.
Light, light is your reward!
Scilla and Bloodroot, lift up you heads
From cowering under winter's weight.
Delicate the early morning light.
Fresh and translucent
As the flesh of adolescence.
I fling myself upon the earth
Sucking up the new blood of nature
Into my bones.
I run laughing down the hills,
Trailing gossamer woodland scent.
I lie exhausted 'neath a tree
To sleep off the hot-buttered rum
Of the sun.
The sweet, sweet smell of the grass
I remember last.

1969
Friends Journal

Early Leaves

Early leaves
How Japanese!
Tender parasols upon the trees,
Hok'sai-drawn.

1969

The Gloxinia

With what grace
You fade away, lovely bloom,
Leaving room in the eye
Of the beloved beholder
For the young buds just coming on.
Finally, of course, you
Will drop, one by one,
Until the beloved beholder
Gently breaks the dropped and
Broken petals, leaving room
For the fresh, young buds
To speak again of the beauty.
Long, too long, forgotten.

1969

Dust of a Million Stars

Dust of a million stars
Fall down upon me
And leave me again
With wholeness.

1970

Sustenance

I love the little buds just peeking out.
They invariably ask
The stranger just passing by,
"Which way the sun?"

1971
Friends Journal

Perpetual Sorrow

Soughing of pines,
Do you feel the pain
Of the lost poets
Of the world?
Do you perpetually weep
For unsung songs?
Or are you the soul-cry
Of Muses upspent,
Looking for masters
In the back alleys of time
So distant
From your own perpetual testament
To keep throttled sighs
From perishing utterly?

1980

Symposium

The wind in the willow is a symphony
Whose calm fronds wave in synchrony.
When you see it
Don't think of me
But sway to it diastolically, diaphrasing harmony*

So then forever you shall be
A joy in the soul
Of a willow tree
Who played in private
But not for thee.

*"Diaphrase" means that in the midst of a an action between two beings the
harmony of the rhythm between them can be raised in a precise way to a new
level.

1985

REALITIES

Two Commentaries on Modern Man's Self-Image

A dog dreams of chasing a hare
While man, on the other hand,
Chases a star
Down the staircase of time
Where, along the way,
Possibilities become eventualities
And are more, therefore,
Than a dog's dream.

• • •

Return, naked ape, from examining
Your genitals – a child's play –
And rest your head on the pillow
Of a cloud which reveals
In its turn the diadem
Of your birthright.
Claim it quickly, O Man,
Before it is considered
Perfectly natural for Man
To have intercourse
With the apes.
You already see the shape
Of such creation
And shudder in your sleep.
The first few shudders
Awaken the Creation
And it waits, trembling,
For your decision.

1965

Lost Innocence

At what point can you no longer speak
With the authority of innocence
Nor roar in righteousness
As the young lion?
Who has retained or regained it
Through suffering and sacrifice purged
Of double-dealing and self-defense?

It is not the great moment when we lose it.
But the compilation of small compromises
That saps the heart and stops the eye
From looking right on.
We build the prison little by little
Until we no longer even perceive
The line between good and evil
That was so clear in our passionate youth.
The substitute for authority is to pretend
To be wise, to view all sides,
To be dispassionate,
When in truth we are without spirit.
No wonder the young turn away.
What have they to learn
But the art of silence in crisis,
The cold eye of the serpent
Who glides noiselessly away
When the dust is up?

1970

The American Way of Life

Here in America,
Caught in the trap of technology,
We send our flares to the spirit world,
Hoping for redemption in a fortnight.

1970

Can the Intelligent ever enjoy Life?

Can the very intelligent ever enjoy life
With those everlasting comparisons
At the astringency of perpetual paradoxes?
Can they nuzzle the earth stuff
Without wanting to make a poem about it?
Do they flay passion with the stiletto
Of objective objections
Till it lies flopping on the cutting board
Like a cold fish?
Do they see a cloud ever
Without saying, "it is like"?
Is infinitesimal dissection
A coronary disease
Caused by the perpetual palpitation
Of the cerebellum?
Or does the constant exercise of the mind
Train the passions with telescopic sight
On some gossamer goal
Far away and inconceivable
To the lusty and broad-bottomed?

1981
Primipara

The Eye Beyond Hiroshima
(A Memorium in a Satellite a Billion Light Years Away)

"O I Am, to whom will the wind sing of it
As the earth spins empty, moaning,
Into the far reaches of time beyond tomorrow?
No one will weep. A charnal house is silent.
Blackened bones and a child's eyeball do not cry.
A dust cloud is shroud,
Shielding desolation from the inquiring eye of the sun
As it dumbly utters farewell
To its once green and golden companion,
Torn from her old orbit, habitual rounds of the eons,
Where she paced orderly and lawful,
Mother to generations who nursed in her fruitful womb
But who, in the tenth month, were torn raging from her
By a hand not born of woman
But alien and strange. (Whence?)
This creature, all great devouring eye,
A Cyclops,
In blind and bleeding fury, groping in its cave for light,
Ends its days of agony by its own hand."
"Mother, death is the final relief,
Silence a solution after all.
Better resolution by suicide than the desolation
Of never finally knowing, with its pitched, cold,
Frenzy,
Poised like a poignard of ice,
In the center of the great brain.
Isn't that right, Mother?"

The Eye Beyond Hiroshima
(A Memorium in a Satellite a Billion Light Years Away *cont.*)

("O the winds of time sweep 'round the curves
Of the universe
But they do not cry like we of the womb do .
Where art Thou, O Lord, where,
As the weathervane on our homely housetop
Points north?")
"The allegory of the cave
Will never then be resolved.
My child.
Who will ponder?"

"Is our only hope then, Mother,
That our dust
Will form a new star?"

"Dust, my child?
What dust?"

Finis

1983

The Eye Beyond Hiroshima
(The Lament of the Fallen Steward)

Fate rolls inexorably on
Not to be fooled by any of us
Who, nevertheless, stare at it with eye
Dark as Horror!

We run to hold up the sky
With tiny hands
And the heavens roar with laughter
And drift on by.

And when we are weary with gazing into space
And turn our eyes downward to our feet,
Mired in the night,
We discern that our path is a treadmill after all.

I say goodbye in silence
Through the mist of an inner vision
To the face of my friend who is so beloved
And I say to myself,
"She's lucky that she's so old
And will soon go
To a field flowered in as-old-a-hope."

And the once-warm clouds,
The splendid, brave trees,
Stalwart and oblivious as always
Of all but the coming spring,
I view with the sorrow of parting.
To the small squirrel who sits up so boldly
Staring at me, wondering as of old,
I say that "I'm sorry"
(Which is the old, repeated, lie as is always
our reply!)

The Eye Beyond Hiroshima
(The Lament of the Fallen Steward *cont.*)

My heart is pain
For the fate of all innocence
At the hand
Of the fallen steward.

I look at it a moment,
A perfect work of art,
And I beg the artist
To send us someone again.
In answer, an autumn leaf falls at my feet,
Sere and curled with grief
Like hope at this,
The end of our season of grace.

1984

Elegy for Nusi
September 17, 1984

Sudden Silence.
Then a nexus of pain when we pass to and fro
Dreamlike before a mirror of the impossible
Searching for escape, but there is none.

Late in the day, I, still stunned, saw to my surprise
The young men move as always
Against the too-vivid-background
Of the common day gone by on time.

Then night with its far cries.
And again the sunrise against
My disbelief at its regularity.

Only then did I realize how I have ever moved
With you in the backdrop of my sinews

And, in the shifting motions of time
I thought the world, too,
Ought to have stopped with the shock.

It did, of course, with your sudden silence
And will move on again only when impossible
Drops its prefix slowly, slowly,
In the cathedral haze of the autumn light.

1984

RANDOM

Where Was I?

Where was I
When the wind was high?
In hiding?
Out, out
Lest I die by degrees
Instead of at once
At my post.

1965

Retrospective Evocation

Retrospective evocation is not equivocal.
Though convoluted,
It is neat what it picks of the past
As necessary now.

1969

Verification

I sink in the ocean,
Gasping, gagging, terrified:
But I keep a translucent eye
On the stars.
If they drown, one by one,
As I am,
I shall be gone,
Never to return.

1970

The Chicken and the Hen

Where do we go from here?
Said the chicken to the hen.
From here to then
Said the hen.

1976

Whispering

To accept ambivalence
Is hard for me.
I'm purist at heart.
I cannot accept compromise with grace,
Can you?

Together, then, let us lay bare,
In the teeth of ill winds,
The tough root of purity
That connects us so daringly
With perfection.

1970

The Sunflower

Like the slow-swinging sunflower
Turning with the light
As the sun rides on past the meridian
Toward the West
Is my soul.
My soul is like the slow-swinging searchlight
Probing the night
Until its beam homes in on the sunflower
Safe in her nocturnal rest.

1970

A Child's Heart

A child's heart is delicate as spring.
It breaks easily
Like lilacs in late snow.
It is mortally wounded
By the slightest offense.
Therefore, gaze seriously
Into wide blue eyes,
Remembering how it was
When your early bloom
Was crushed by the cruelest of all,
A late frost.

1970

Acceptance

Deck me with sunlight
I am born anew.
The forms of today
Are my species,
The clay for tomorrow's remembrance.

1970
Friends Journal

Swaying

Persuaded that genesis never occurred,
I sway in the oscillating jellies
Of in-between beliefs.
I cannot throw myself
Whole-heartedly
One way or the other.
I need fear or love
To make me move
Toward some promised, still center
Or, at least, some garden congenial
To the undecided.

1972

Present Tense

Fantasy lifts you
In its arms of dreams.
Where are you now?
The vantage point disappears
And you float in the cobweb of illusion.
Finding your way back is hard
For your memory serves only the fantasy
And not the wind in the trees
Which is real.

1972

Nameless Wayfarers

Nameless wayfarers by the side of the sea
What do you look for in the salt brine,
A new ship sailing
Or an old one departing from known parts?
Or do you seek the wind
To cleanse a troubled heart?
Or the gulls' cry
To snatch away your wasted soul?
Or the roll and hiss of the tide
In which to sink world-weary feet?
Do you seek healing in the depthless sea
As only the old waters can give it?
You have come to the right place
For the ocean gives freely
Surcease from sorrow,
Its own and yours buried with the bones at the bottom,
There a treasure trove forever of forgotten woes.

1972

The Shadow-Pool

Poetry flows through me
Under my heart.
It draws on the shadow-pool
Of my soul.
Nameless wayfarer
In subterranean caverns,
Erupt again in a shower of jewels
And lave me whole
In your falling, falling of song.

1972

Guilt

Fay are the flowers of the heart.
Alluvial soil has eluded them.
Gnarled, twisted, wine-dark,
They are vines rather than petals.
As age becomes hoar-headed.
They strangle the last apertures
And I know with final agony
That my heart attack is cerebral.

1974

A Wind-Blown Child

Bent with age,
My brain is stuffed with chaff.
Gale, blow through my sails
That I might spring up
Quick as a dandelion,
Again a wind-blown child.

1972

A Birthday Salutation

Dear friend of fifty years,
Frank, straightforward,
Angry at my transgressions,
You bend always on my side
With love.
I have trusted you long.
In the dim dawn,
The hells of night.
Filled with the guilt of too many betrayals,
You were there in my heart.
Real, I could come to you with all thoughts,
All tears, all joys, open my soul.

Your life leaves a trace of God in mine.
I see you bending to His will
And I envy your obedience;
I am too refractory.
But it is silenced in your presence.
You lead me upward
And I will treasure you forever
For the bonds of love were made
Before we were.

1974

For Gladys on the Death of Her Husband, Howard

He is dead.
O the sorrow.
The great, ballooning, sorrow of it.
But they tell me
To bend with the blow.
What they cannot know
Is how slow, how slow it is,
Upright again.

1975

For Women Only/A Love Song

Our slow-stirring pools run deep
Under the sparkling, paper-thin, surface
Which reflects the moon.
But a slow-moving madrigal
Brings the sun around again
To pierce the gloomy depths
With one shaft of light.
And that shaft of light
Explodes into incandescence
To light our way home
To our native air.

1975

From a Sister Bereaved

A solemn and sweet soul
Was my sister,
Gone now beyond recall.
She floats in the deeps of her dream
Like an old and fragrant rose
Until nature, with its charmed tentacles,
Draws her back again earthward,
This time queen of her life,
Lost, O never more.
She has suffered too much for that.
Let her live, let her love.
Let her be free.
Bathed in innocence of beginning.

1976

Pole Stars

There are some natures (neither named nor famous)
Too noble – in themselves self-contained –
For ordinary intercourse with friends.
These mighty souls need no completion
Nor consolation at times bereaved
Or ambition thwarted.
They bear all in themselves,
Expecting no surcease from ceaseless care
And disdaining any touch of mortal warmth,
Even from others, equal to them,
In solemn pride and beauty.
These face each other like columns of a Grecian temple.
They shine like pole stars.
Never moving, never moved, sternly stationary.
Fixed from time's beginning
That other luminaries, lesser men,
May chart their course by them,
Trembling and exalted.

1977

My Elegant and Ivory Aunts

My elegant and ivory aunts,
Three graces of old porcelain,
With piercing eyes
And pointed minds
Whose old rules of etiquette and grace
Were well defined.
How I remember them with veneration.

One once tartly said:
"Violence varies inversely
With the price of virtue."

Another gentler one observed
One November holiday:
"The ring of suffering
Brings always every absolution."

The third, curly-haired and saucy-nosed,
Lilting naughty as a little chickadee:
"What a gay joke,
Dreaming of love,
Life is."

I was inclined to smile
At these easy words,
Born of wealth they were,
Secure and safe,
Forgetting that war had swirled
'Round them, too.
Using no excuse
For change of character,
Living through it all
Unbent,
They pierced through their experience
With thought,
Shaped it to their wills
And left a heritage of strength
That might yet redeem me
From begging off my duty
With the excuse: "It's more than I can bear."

My Elegant and Ivory Aunts *cont.*

My elegant and ivory aunts,
Three graces of old porcelain,
With piercing eyes
And pointed minds,
Their jewels perfect
Every time!

1982

Out of the Winds of the Memory of the Long, Long, Grasses spins a Paean of Faith

As we pace down the long, long, staircase of time,
Winding slowly, ever more slowly, thank God,
We perceive that the personnae appear
On time and in order.

They are, after all, only the studied tinctures ever dropping
onto the reflecting pool of the mind of Who (Ask the Jew)?
And, it is with the deepest pleasure
That we pause awhile on each landing,
Lean against the balustrades and peering
Out the clearing window of our mind
Into the beauty and comfort of rain,
Look long, watch and listen to:
1) the style of the patter which inevitably leads
   (peripatetically, however) to
2) further distinctions in parallel patter as we all sing a
   veritable circlet of roundelays to our mutual joy
And then go on about our business afterward,
Shimmering in the old, remembered, wonder!

1984

Lullaby for Leleiah

Be still for
The night sings and
Listening,
We wait,
Expectant.

1985

BIOGRAPHY

Joyce Wuesthoff Povolny was born on December 23, 1929, in Milwaukee, Wisconsin. Her father was a businessman. She was educated for secondary school at a private school and then went on to Connecticut College for Women for a BA and to Haverford Quaker College, Philadelphia for an MA. She worked for the American Friends Service Committee in Philadelphia and then went to Japan with her husband Mojmir Povolny in 1956 to work in the workcamp program in Tokyo. They then went to Chicago where she joined the Evanston Meeting of Friends in 1958. From there they went to Appleton, Wisconsin, where her husband taught for 29 years at Lawrence University. They have two sons, David and Daniel. She has been active all her life in the League of Women Voters and various charitable organisations. She is presently employed on a voluntary basis with a small charitable agency called Leaven.